LET'S PLAY
POKÉMON

This Book Belongs to

My favourite
Poké pal is:

My favourite
Pokémon
game is:

WHO WILL THEIR POKÉMON PARTNER BE?

DESIGN YOUR TRAINER!

Pokémon™

Then and...

Gen 1
GAMES:
Red, Blue, Green (Japan) and Yellow

★ Back in 1996, the first-ever Pokémon games, Red and Green, landed on the Nintendo GameBoy. The Blue version hit the shelves next, quickly followed by the special edition, Pokémon Yellow. These games introduced us to the Kanto region and the first 151 Pokémon!

Gen 3
GAMES:
Ruby, Sapphire and Emerald

★ The third instalment in the series didn't just bring us new games and a whole bunch of new Pokémon, but it also brought us the first remakes, revisiting Gen 1's Kanto in FireRed and LeafGreen! These remakes became the second best-selling GameBoy Advance games, with Ruby and Sapphire at the top!

START HERE!

1 **2** **3** **4** **5**

Gen 2
GAMES:
Gold, Silver and Crystal

★ Welcome to Johto! As well as 100 new Pokémon to discover, these games also brought some key additions to the series, including Dark and Steel types and shiny Pokémon. They also introduced gender, breeding and baby 'Mon, too like Pichu!

Gen 4
GAMES:
Diamond, Pearl and Platinum

★ You might have visited Sinnoh (or Hisui) in Brilliant Diamond, Shining Pearl, or Legends: Arceus, but gamers were first introduced to this region back in 2006! This gen also gave us two new remakes – HeartGold and SoulSilver.

GUIDE TO POKÉMON!

TAKE A PIKA THESE GAMES!

Now!

Gen 5
GAMES:

Black, White, Black 2 and White 2

★ Instead of a special version, Gen 5 introduced sequels with a brand-new story for the first time in the series. On top of this they added 156 new 'Mon, taking the total to a massive 649!

Gen 7
GAMES:

Sun, Moon, Ultra Sun and Ultra Moon

★ These games took us to the Alola region and introduced us to regional forms, giving some of our fave 'Mon a new look! Then in 2018, Pokémon landed on the Switch for the first time with the Gen 1 remakes, Let's Go Pikachu and Let's Go Eevee. These not only tied in with Pokémon GO, but they also had an awesome Poké Ball controller!

Gen 6
GAMES:

X and Y

★ The first core series games to hit the 3DS, X and Y introduced Fairy-type 'Mon, changing the typing of faves like Clefairy and Togepi! Plus, this gen brought back remasters with Omega Ruby and Alpha Sapphire.

Gen 8
GAMES:

Sword and Shield

DON'T WOBBLE, PICK SOBBLE!

★ Gen 8 delivered a lotta firsts, from Sword and Shield's open-world Wild Area, to Expansion Pass DLC, to brand-new battle mechanics in the spin-off game, Pokémon Legends: Arceus! We were even treated to remasters of Diamond and Pearl, with a chibi art style.

Gen 9
GAMES:

Scarlet and Violet

★ Not only has it introduced us to new 'Mon like Sprigatitio, Fuecoco and Quaxly, the latest instalment in the core series has also introduced some brand-new, game-changing mechanics! With an open-world region and four-player multiplayer, the way we play Pokémon will never be the same!

WHAT'S YOUR FAVOURITE POKÉMON GENERATION?

ULTIMATE SUPER STARTERS!

SPECIAL MENTION

EEVEE

GEN: 1 **TYPE:** NORMAL

★ Although not a true core-series starter, Eevee is an epic partner Pokémon in the Let's Go games!

28

SOBBLE

GEN: 8 **TYPE:** WATER

★ This timid little 'Mon can camouflage itself whenever it's nervous! Plus, its tears are said to make others cry and have the same effect as chopping 100 onions!

27

POPPLIO

GEN: 7 **TYPE:** WATER

★ Although its final evolution Primarina's additional Fairy-typing helps it to pack a punch, we'd love to see more powerful water attacks from this 'Mon.

26

CHIKORITA

GEN: 2 **TYPE:** GRASS

★ This sun-loving Pokémon might have the best overall base stats out of the other Gen 2 starters, but its evolutions, Bayleef and Meganium, struggle to make too much of an impact at Johto's gyms!

25
SNIVY

GEN: 5 **TYPE:** GRASS

★ Snivy uses sunlight to power-up its speed, making it the fastest of all the Gen 5 starters! Although it's the fastest, it also has the lowest HP, and its tail starts to droop when it's not feeling well.

24
QUAXLY

GEN: 9 **TYPE:** WATER

★ Paldea's **Duckling Pokémon**, Quaxly, **uses its powerful legs for swimming and kicking opponents, but it has a habit of overthinking everything and hates when its feathers get dirty!**

23
CHESPIN

GEN: 6 **TYPE:** GRASS

★ This Kalos cutie uses the thick wooden shell on its head and back to protect itself from attacks. Chespin's curious and cheeky nature has also been known to get it into trouble!

22
PIPLUP

GEN: 4 **TYPE:** WATER

★ This proud Penguin Pokémon can take a while to bond with humans and doesn't always listen to its Trainer, but its final evolution, Empoleon, is honoured by the people of Hisui and known as Master of the Waves!

21
SCORBUNNY

GEN: 8 **TYPE: FIRE**

★ Scorbunny runs to prepare for battle, building up fire inside its body. The special pads on the soles of its feet get so hot that a single kick can burn an opponent or even start a fire!

20
TOTODILE

GEN: 2 **TYPE: WATER**

★ Although Totodile might be a playful Pokémon at heart, its strong jaws, sharp teeth, and love of biting can be a bit dangerous – Trainers better watch out!

19
TEPIG

GEN: 5 **TYPE: FIRE**

★ This little piggy went to Unova! Tepig can use its fiery snout for everything from roasting berries to shooting fireballs at opponents!

18
OSHAWOTT

GEN: 5 **TYPE: WATER**

★ As well as being a starter Pokémon in the Black and White games, you can also pick Oshawott as your companion for your adventures in Legends: Arceus, too. It even has a special Hisuian evolution!

17
TURTWIG
GEN: 4 **TYPE:** GRASS

★ You can tell a lot about a Turtwig from its trusty shell! A healthy Turtwig will have a moist shell and seedling on its head but when it's thirsty, the leaf will droop.

16
FENNEKIN
GEN: 6 **TYPE:** FIRE

★ Fennekin, the Fire Fox Pokémon, loves to munch on twigs for energy. As it evolves into Delphox it develops Psychic abilities and instead of snacking on sticks it uses one as a flame-tipped magic wand!

15
TREECKO
GEN: 3 **TYPE:** GRASS

★ This cool climber is rarely found in the wild but can sometimes be spotted living high in the trees in overgrown forests. In fact, Treecko's so protective over its territory, it's known as a protector of the forests!

14
FUECOCO
GEN: 9 **TYPE:** FIRE

★ Paldea's fave Fire Croc, Fuecoco, might be a bit slow and laid-back but with a high HP and a strong Special Attack it's a force to be reckoned with!

13 LITTEN

GEN: 7 **TYPE: FIRE**

★ This fiery kitty spends time alone and is slow to trust others. It prefers to spend time grooming, saving up fur in its stomach for flaming furballs!

12 SQUIRTLE

GEN: 1 **TYPE: WATER**

★ One of the most iconic Water-types of all, Squirtle is a great partner pick! Plus, its evolution Blastoise's water cannons are a seriously cool upgrade!

11 CYNDAQUIL

GEN: 2 **TYPE: FIRE**

★ One of the Johto region's starter trio, Cyndaquil is a Fire Mouse whose flames grow more powerful the angrier it gets!

10 GROOKEY

GEN: 8 **TYPE: GRASS**

★ Grookey is one musical monkey! The stick in its hair isn't just used for attacks, it can also be used as a special drumstick that helps flowers and grass to grow, as well as healing some plant-like 'Mon!

9 BULBASAUR

GEN: 1 **TYPE:** GRASS POISON

★ Number one in the Pokédex, Bulbasaur is one of the only dual-type starters around! The bulb on its back indicates when it's going to evolve by flashing blue!

8 CHIMCHAR

GEN: 4 **TYPE:** FIRE

★ This Chimp's fiery tail is fuelled by gas from its belly! As Chimchar evolves, the flames turn into an awesome crown of fire that never goes out!

7 SPRIGATITO

★ This clean kitty regularly grooms its face to keep its special fur moist. This helps it absorb energy from the sunlight to power-up its Grass-type attacks!

GEN: 9 **TYPE:** GRASS

6 CHARMANDER

GEN: 1 **TYPE:** FIRE

★ We love Charmander on its own, but the fact that it evolves into one of the coolest Pokémon of all-time, Charizard, cements its place as a top Fire-starter.

5 TORCHIC

GEN: 3 **TYPE: FIRE**

★ Thanks to a flame that burns inside its body, when you give Torchic a cuddle it'll be nice and toasty. But watch out – it can also breathe fireballs that leave opponents scorched black!

4 ROWLET

GEN: 7 **TYPE: GRASS FLYING**

★ What's not to love about Rowlet?! Its type combo makes it a well-rounded competitor but add in its solid stats and you've got a superstar starter!

3 MUDKIP

GEN: 3 **TYPE: WATER**

★ When Mudkip evolves it becomes a dual Water/Ground-type, reducing its weaknesses. This, combined with awesome moves, high HP and strong attack stats, makes Mudkip a future powerhouse!

2 PIKACHU

GEN: 1 **TYPE: ELECTRIC**

★ The most famous Pokémon of them all, Pikachu is a perfect partner! Whether you're going retro with Pokémon Yellow or adventuring in Let's Go, with Pikachu by your side, you're bound to have a good time!

1 FROAKIE

GEN: 6 **TYPE: WATER**

★ If you're looking for a top-tier offensive 'Mon, Froakie's final evolution, Greninja, is the one for you! It even has a special Ash-Greninja form to take your battles to the next level!

SPOT THE DIFFERENCE

There are six differences between these two Pokémon pictures. Can you catch 'em all?

CATCH 'EM ALL!

Collect a Poké Ball every time you spot a difference!

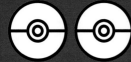

ANSWERS:

PALDEA PATH PICKER!

WHERE WILL YOUR TREASURE HUNT TAKE YOU?

CAN'T DECIDE WHAT STORY TO FOLLOW IN POKÉMON VIOLET AND SCARLET? USE YOUR FINGER TO TRACE YOUR WAY TO TREASURE!

1

2

3

4

VICTORY ROAD

YOU'RE GOING OLD SCHOOL! YOU CHOSE TO CLIMB TO THE VERY TOP OF THE POKÉMON LEAGUE! YOU'LL BATTLE YOUR FRIEND (OR RIVAL) NEMONA AND TAKE ON AMAZING GYM LEADERS TO SWEEP UP THOSE BADGES!

PATH OF LEGENDS

YOU'LL WORK WITH ARVEN TO TAKE ON TITANS, POKÉMON THAT HAVE BEEN SUPERCHARGED BY HERBA MYSTICA! YOU'LL LEARN A LOT ABOUT KORAIDON AND MIRAIDON, AND YOU'LL CERTAINLY NEVER GO HUNGRY!

STARFALL STREET

THIS STORYLINE WILL SEE YOU TAKE ON TEAM STAR WITH OPERATION STARFALL! YOU'LL INFILTRATE TEAM STAR BASES AND TAKE ON GRUNTS, BOSSES AND STARMOBILES, ALL WHILE UNCOVERING THE TRUTH BEHIND TEAM STAR!

GO YOUR OWN WAY

INSTEAD OF FOCUSING ON ONE PATH, YOU'LL TRY THEM ALL OUT! MAYBE YOU'LL COMPLETE YOUR POKÉDEX, OR EXPLORE THE VAST EXPANSES OF PALDEA. WE'RE SURE YOU'LL FIND YOUR TREASURE IN THE END!

Be the very best, like no one ever was, with our map of Kanto!

ALL ABOUT KANTO!

PEWTER CITY
- This is where you'll get your first gym badge! Can you beat Brock and his Onix?

VIRIDIAN FOREST
- A good spot for catching bugs, but secretly also a good place to find a Pikachu as well!

PALLET TOWN
- This is where it all starts with Professor Oak! Will you take Bulbasaur, Charmander, or Squirtle? Or maybe you're more into Pikachu or Eevee?

CINNABAR ISLAND
- Cinnabar Island is mostly a volcano! In some games, it's home to the Fire-type gym leader, Blaine. You should visit wha left of the Pokémon Mansion, if you want to learn about Pokémon clonir

CERULEAN CAVE
● Once you're the Champion, you can come here and catch legendary Pokémon Mewtwo!

POWER PLANT
● Based on Japan's first ever nuclear power plant, this electrifying location is home to Zapdos!

POKÉMON TOWER
● A graveyard where Trainers put their Pokémon to rest. Ghosts have been scaring Trainers away. Can you help?

VERMILION CITY
● Home to Lt. Surge and his Raichu. It's also Kanto's sea port! You can take a trip on the S.S. Anne, or use the Seagallop Ferries to go to the Sevii Islands from here.

WHO'S WHO?

Get to know some of Kanto's local heroes!

BROCK

★ The Pewter City Gym Leader! He uses Rock-type Pokémon like Geodude. If you can beat him, he'll give you the Boulder Badge.

MISTY

MAKE A SPLASH!

★ Misty focuses on attacking moves and Water-type Pokémon, and is the Cerulean City Gym Leader. The strongest member of her team is Starmie – watch out for its Bubble Beam!

LT. SURGE

★ The Lightning Lieutenant! Before Surge was the Vermilion City Gym Leader, he was a soldier. As you might expect from his name, he uses Electric-type Pokémon, including a powerful Raichu.

LET'S GET STARTED!

Get to know the Gen 1 starters!

PIKACHU!

A Mouse that stores electrical currents in its cheeks. If too many are in the same place it can cause a lightning storm!

EEVEE

This cute Evolution Pokémon has a bushy tail and a fluffy collar, and can evolve into lots of different 'Mon!

KANTO

GIOVANNI

TOTALLY BOSS!

AGATHA

LANCE

DRAGON POWER!

★ The boss of Team Rocket is often up to no good, and dreams of world domination through the use of Pokémon power. Surprisingly, he is also the Viridian City Gym Leader.

★ The spookiest (and oldest) member of Kanto's Elite Four! She has also known Professor Oak since they were very young, and felt betrayed when he gave up battling.

★ Champion of the Indigo League. He is a Dragon Master, and considers them virtually indestructible. He also has a collection of identical fancy capes that he buys from the Celadon Department Store.

BULBASAUR

Scientists aren't sure if Bulbasaur's a plant or an animal, but they're known to be extremely loyal!

CHARMANDER

A little Lizard Pokémon with a fire on the end of its tail. If the fire ever goes out, it will die!

SQUIRTLE

A Tiny Turtle, with the tail of a squirrel. It can spray water and hide in its shell at the same time!

POKÉMON™ Let's GO

BOARD GAME!

EXPLORE KANTO AND BECOME THE POKÉMON CHAMPION!

ALL YOU NEED:

★ A dice
★ Coins or buttons to use as counters

START

1 — PALLET TOWN

ROUTE 1

2

3 — You have to deliver a parcel to professor Oak. Go back to start!

4 — VIRIDIAN CITY

5 — VIRIDIAN FOREST

6 — You get lost in the forest! Miss a turn!

7 — PEWTER CITY

8 — MT. MOON

9 — You hitch a ride on an Onix. Roll again!

11

13 — ROUTE 5

12 — Misty's Starmie is too strong! Go back two spaces.

14 — VERMILION CITY

15 — You defeated Lt. Surge! Go aboard to S.S. Anne to celebrate!

16

S.S. ANNE

ROUTE 11

17

18 — Snorlax is blocking the path! Take Diglett's Cave back to Pewter City.

19 — ROCK TUNNEL

TOP TEN MOVIES!

THESE POKÉMON MOVIES ARE THE VERY BEST!

7

POKÉMON THE MOVIE: VOLCANION AND THE MECHANICAL MARVEL (2016)

When Volcanion tries to rescue the artificial Pokémon Magearna, a strange force binds it to Ash. Although Volcanion hates humans, it has no choice but to take Ash along for the ride!

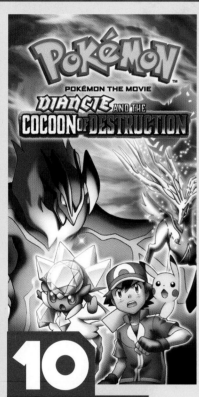

9

POKÉMON 3: THE MOVIE (2000)

From mind-bending Pokémon, to the mysterious Unown, Ash, Brock and Misty – with a little help from Team Rocket – face one of their biggest ever challenges in this awesome movie.

10

POKÉMON THE MOVIE: DIANCIE AND THE COCOON OF DESTRUCTION (2014)

Ash and friends must keep the mythical Diancie safe as she sets out to find Xerneas and make a Heart Diamond to save her home!

8

POKÉMON THE MOVIE 2000 (1999)

In order to bring balance back to the Orange Islands, Ash must collect each of the three spheres of Fire, Ice and Lightning!

6

POKÉMON THE MOVIE: HOOPA AND THE CLASH OF AGES (2015)

With the threat of an ancient Pokémon returning to wreak havoc on the world, Ash must step up and save the day... or else!

5 POKÉMON THE MOVIE: THE POWER OF US (2018)

Ash and the residents of Fula City need to come together and put things right to save their home town when their annual Wind Festival comes under threat!

4 POKÉMON: LUCARIO AND THE MYSTERY OF MEW (2005)

Guided by Lucario, Ash and the gang set out to find Pikachu who was taken to the Tree of Beginnings by Mew!

3 POKÉMON THE MOVIE: I CHOOSE YOU! (2017)

This re-telling of Ash's first adventure is epic! On his 10th birthday, Ash receives his first-ever Pokémon and sets about the adventure of a lifetime.

2 POKÉMON DETECTIVE PIKACHU (2019)

In the first live-action Pokémon movie, Tim is the only person who can hear the coffee-loving Detective Pikachu speak! They must work together to solve the mystery of Tim's missing dad!

1 POKÉMON: THE FIRST MOVIE – MEWTWO STRIKES BACK (1998)

It might be over 20 years old, but the first-ever Pokémon movie still makes us cry every time! When scientists try to create the ultimate Pokémon weapon, Mewtwo, things go horribly wrong and Ash is forced to put himself in danger to save Pokémon everywhere!

LIGHTS OUT!

A GROUP OF GAMING HEROES HAVE SNUCK INTO RHYME CITY! CAN YOU HELP DETECTIVE PIKACHU FIND OUT WHO'S HIDING IN THE DARK?

2
A GOLD RING IF YOU GUESS ME SUPER-FAST!

1
THIS IS ROYALLY DIFFICULT!

3
OH, BROTHER! WHO COULD THIS BE?

4
WHO IS CRASHING AROUND IN THE DARKNESS?

5
TAKE A DEEP BREATH BEFORE YOU TRY TO GUESS!

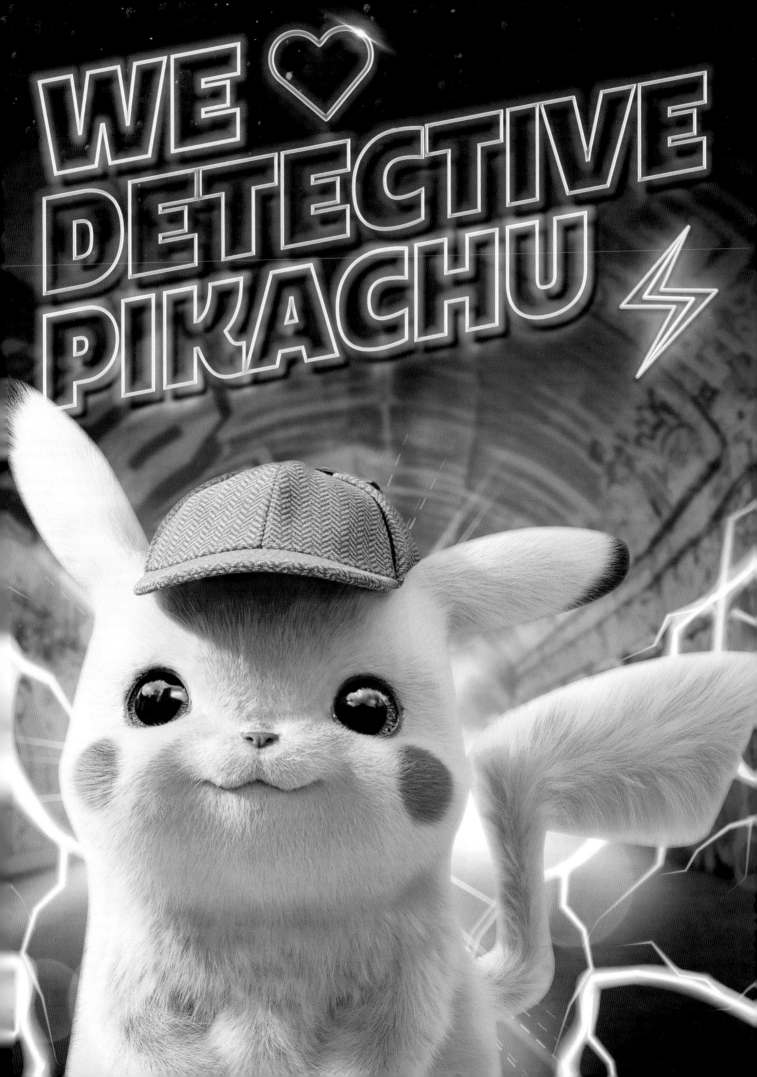

GREAT GAME!

Platform: Nintendo 3DS
Released: 2016

This awesome puzzle/adventure game introduced us to Pikachu like we'd never seen them before! Play as Tim and team-up with Detective Pikachu to explore scenes, search for clues and uncover mysteries.

MUST-SEE MOVIE!

Released: 2019

The first-ever live-action Pokémon movie hit the big screens back in 2019 and has stayed in our hearts ever since! Seeing Pikachu and other 'Mon brought to life in the hustle and bustle of Rhyme City was incredible – we hope there's more movies like this in the future!

SUPER SEQUEL!

A sequel to the epic Detective Pikachu 3DS game is in the works! Although details of this new game are still top secret, we know it'll follow on from the original game's story and will land on the Nintendo Switch in the near future. We can't wait!

DETECTIVE
PIKACHU™
PUZZLES!

CAN YOU HELP DETECTIVE PIKACHU SOLVE THESE TRICKY POKÉMON PUZZLES?

ULTIMATE POKÉMON!

We've created the ultimate Pokémon – can you tell where each of the Pokémon have been used?

SOLVE THE MYSTERIES WITH ME!

CHARIZARD ▸ ☐

SLOWBRO ┄┄┄▸ ☐

ARTICUNO ┄┄▸ ☐

SPOT THE DIFFERENCE!

Can you spot five differences between these two pictures?

POKÉMON HUNT!

Piplup has gotten lost in the fountain – help Detective Pikachu find him!

START

ARCEUS BATTLE!

The ULTIMATE test of a trainer!

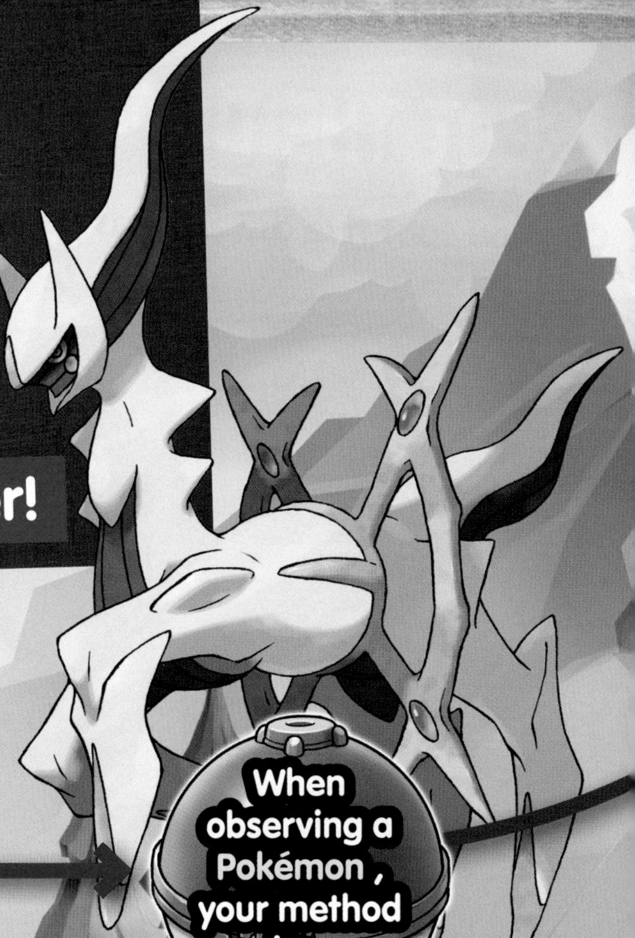

START!

A Pokémon attacks you...

Flee from danger

When observing a Pokémon, your method is...

Stay and fight

Quick and direct

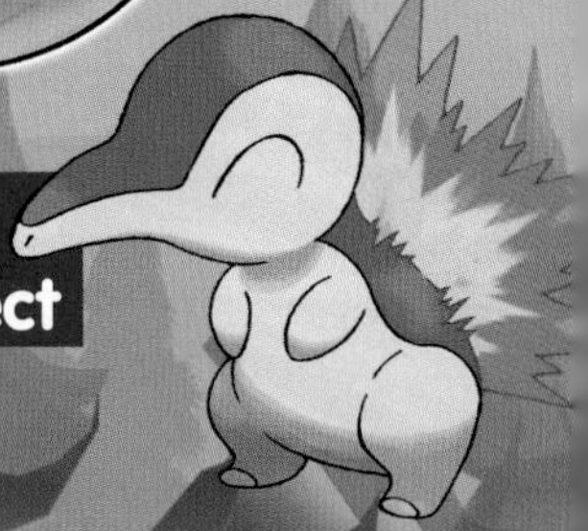

How are your throwing skills?

My aim is true

How organised are you?

A bit clumsy

Exploring new areas

Leppa Berry

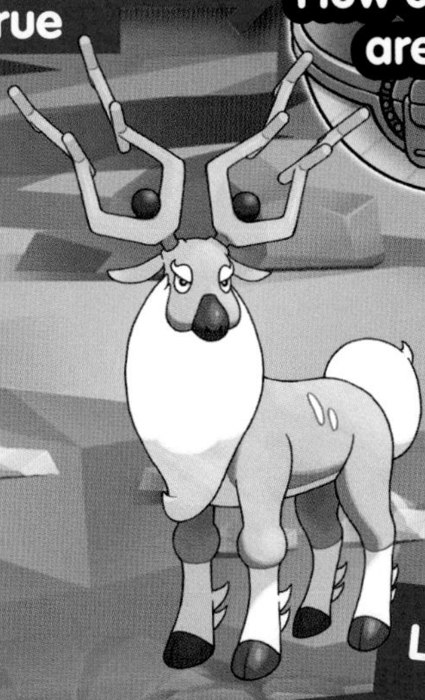

Which berry would you bring to battle?

Nanab Berry

POKÉMON CONQUEST

MASTER STRATEGY

● Pokémon Conquest is a strategy RPG that brings real Japanese historical figures and Pokémon together in the Ransei region for one awesome adventure!

CASTLE COMBAT

● Ransei is shaped like an Arceus, and is divided up into 17 sub-regions, each of which has its own castle to conquer! Can you beat them all?

HUMAN EVOLUTION

● Conquest is the only game in the Pokémon series where the human characters get experience points and transform just like their partners!

DID YOU KNOW?

POKÉMON CONQUEST WAS TURNED INTO A COMIC BOOK IN JAPAN!

RELEASE: 2012   PLATFORM: NINTENDO DS

DID YOU KNOW?

Impress your mates with these Poké facts!

SO SPARKLY!

Pikachu's name is a mash-up of two Japanese sound words! The 'Pika' part comes from 'pikapika' which describes a sparkling sound, and the 'chu' part comes from 'chuchu' which is the noise a mouse makes. So, Pikachu literally means Sparkly Mouse Sound!

SUPER SIZES!

Measuring up at just 10cm each, Flabébé and Cosmoem are two of the smallest Pokémon in existence, but their weights couldn't be more different. In fact, Flabébé is one of the lightest, weighing only 0.1kg, while Cosmoem is almost 1000 times heavier at a whopping 999.9kg!

NO. 1!

Although Bulbasaur is #001 in the Pokédex and Arceus is said to have possibly created the entire Pokémon universe, neither of them were the first-ever Pokémon! That title goes to Rhydon, who was the first 'Mon to be drawn according to game designer, Ken Sugimori.

NEW NAMES!

In the Pokémon Red and Blue beta versions, some 'Mon had totally different names. If you thought Jigglypuff and Wigglytuff were cute already, wait until you hear their original names... Pudding and Custard!

REAL RIVALS!

Pikachu and Meowth are true opposites! As well as being on different sides in the anime series, Meowth's Pokédex number, 52, is the reverse of Pikachu's 25. Plus, they're literally a cat and a mouse!

THE ULTIMATE SUPER SHOWDOWN!

ROUND ONE!

GRENINJA VS. **LUCARIO**

■ We're not holding back with this first battle! This would be a super-close showdown, but when the dust settles, we reckon Lucario would come out on top.

WINNER: LUCARIO

PIKACHU VS. **SNORLAX**

POKÉ-ZZZZZZ...

■ Well, this one's a doozy! We love a nap as much as the next guy but not when you're in a tournament. Pikachu wins this one easily.

WINNER: PIKACHU

SQUIRTLE VS. **CHARMANDER**

■ It's the battle of classic elements! As much as we love Charmander's fiery attitude, it's no match for Squirtle and its water gun!

WINNER: SQUIRTLE

BULBASAUR VS. **EEVEE**

■ Although Bulbasaur's grass powers make it a tough competitor in the jungle or the forest, we reckon Eevee's super-speed would give them the advantage – and the win!

WINNER: EEVEE

ROUND TWO!

PIKACHU VS. **LUCARIO**

■ Now THIS is tough! Pikachu is speedy and shocking, making it a worthy opponent. But Lucario is a tough-as-nails fighter who won't make this an easy fight. We love you Pikachu but Lucario's got this in the bag.

★★★★★★★
WINNER:
★★★★★★★
LUCARIO

SQUIRTLE VS. **EEVEE**

■ Now we've got two fast fighters going head-to-head! Eevee has some cool elemental evolutions but in their base form, their abilities just aren't up to scratch. Squirtle for the win!

★★★★★★★
WINNER:
★★★★★★★
SQUIRTLE

THE FINAL!

LUCARIO VS. SQUIRTLE

■ None of these battles have been easy — well, maybe the Snorlax one was! Squirtle would get mighty close, using all their powerful water abilities to turn the tide. However, Lucario's endurance and versatility would win them the crown!

I DEMAND A RE-MATCH!

CHAMPION: LUCARIO

FIND THAT DITTO!

These Ditto don't want to be caught – but can you catch them all?

EACH DITTO HAS A FACE LIKE THIS!

CAN YOU SPOT?

Meowth | Togedemaru | Pikachu | Vulpix | Jangmo-o | Rowlet

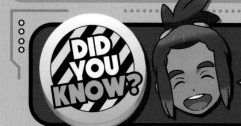

DID YOU KNOW?

Ditto can change how it looks to copy any Pokémon!

ANSWER

POKÉMON

IN REAL LIFE!

MEET THE TOTALLY WILD INSPO FOR YOUR FAVE 'MON!

SUPER SHARK!

POKÉMON:
SHARPEDO

● With strong jaws, sharp teeth and a tall dorsal fin, there's no denying who this 'Mon's real-life lookalike is! The Pokédex states that Sharpedo is sensitive to the smell of blood, just like real great white sharks, who can sniff out a drop of blood from a half a kilometre away!

TURN OVER FOR MORE!

ROARSOME LION!

I AIN'T LION!

POKÉMON: PYROAR

● Just like real lions, male and female Pyroar look totally different! Male Pyroar have majestic manes of red and gold fur that surrounds its face, whereas females have a longer mane that flows down their back. In the wild, lions live in groups called 'prides' – and so do Pyroar!

KOALA CUTIES!

POKÉMON: KOMALA

● Although real-life koalas can sleep for up to 20 hours a day, they're actually nocturnal and most active at night. They might look alike but this sleeping pattern is different from Komala who sleep all day, every day!

GIANT GIRAFFE!

POKÉMON: FARIGIRAF

● Farigiraf might be pretty tall for a regular Pokémon, measuring in at 3.2 metres, but in the world of giraffes, it's not that tall at all! In real life, a giraffe can grow to between 4-6 metres, using its height to keep a lookout for any dangerous predators.

I CAN SEE MY HOUSE FROM HERE!

SNEAKY SALAMANDER!

POKÉMON: SALANDIT

● From its name to its appearance, there's no doubt that Salandit's inspiration comes from the sly salamander. Both creatures are able to release toxins from their bodies to ward off predators and enemies!

TURN OVER FOR MORE POKÉMON IRL!

SWEET SUGAR!

POKÉMON: EMOLGA

● Is it a sugar glider? Is it a flying squirrel? It's Emolga – the Sky Squirrel Pokémon! This Electric/ Flying-type uses the special flap attached to its front legs to glide through the air, just like its real-life lookalikes.

HUGE HIPPO!

POKÉMON: HIPPOPOTAS

● They might look like twins but there's one huge difference between a hippopotamus and their Pokémon pairing: Hippopotas hate water! In the real world, hippos spend most of their day dunked in water to stay cool, but a Hippopotas would much rather burrow in the sand to stay warm!

PANDA POWER!

POKÉMON:
PANCHAM AND PANGORO

● These black-and-white Fighting-type 'Mon might look ferocious, but in real-life pandas are actually shy, generally avoiding habitats near humans. The leaf in Pancham and Pangoro's mouth is a nod to the fact that pandas spend up to 12 hours a day munching on bamboo!

I'M BEAR-Y HUNGRY!

BRILLIANT BEAR!

POKÉMON:
URSARING

● Ursaring have loads in common with their lookalike, the brown bear! Not only do they both have excellent food foraging skills and a taste for berries, nuts and honey, they're also both excellent climbers. In fact, both have even been known to take a nap in the treetops!

WHAT'S YOUR TRAINER TYPE?

WHICH TRAINER TYPE BEST FITS YOUR PERSONALITY?

1 PICK A PASSION...

- (A) HELPING OTHERS! ☑
- (B) BEING THE BEST! ☑
- (C) LEARNING ABOUT THE WORLD. ☑

2 BE HONEST... HOW TIDY IS YOUR ROOM?

- (A) CLEAN, TIDY AND ORGANISED! ☑
- (B) A BIT OF A MESS... ☑
- (C) TOTAL CHAOS... SO. MUCH. STUFF! ☑

3 HOW GOOD ARE YOU AT MULTITASKING?

- (A) SO GOOD, I COULD BE A JUGGLER! ☑
- (B) PRETTY GOOD WHEN I NEED TO. ☑
- (C) I CAN GET A BIT DISTRACTED... ☑

4 YOU'RE TAKING PART IN A RACE. WHAT'S YOUR TACTIC?

- (A) GRAB YOUR FRIENDS AND MAKE IT FUN! ☑
- (B) FOCUS ON THE FINISH LINE! ☑
- (C) JUST ENJOY THE DAY! ☑

5 WHAT'S YOUR DREAM JOB?

- (A) BUSINESS OWNER! ☑
- (B) PROFESSIONAL ATHLETE! ☑
- (C) WORKING WITH ANIMALS! ☑

6 YOU'RE PICKING A FILM FOR TONIGHT. WHAT'S THE GENRE?

- (A) SPORTS. ☑
- (B) MYSTERY. ☑
- (C) ADVENTURE. ☑

IF YOU ANSWERED...

MOSTLY A
GYM LEADER

You're organised, dedicated, and enjoy helping out others – of course you're a Gym Leader! Gym Leaders are great all-rounders who can do well at anything they try, just like you!

MOSTLY B
CHAMPION

You've worked hard to reach the top, beating out the competition to secure your spot as Champion. Champions are masters of combat who aren't afraid of being in the spotlight!

MOSTLY C
COLLECTOR

For you, it's not about where you end up, but the fun you have on the way. Your curious mind makes you passionate about collecting as many 'Mon as you can, just like Collectors!

VICTORY ROAD!

START

IT'S TIME TO BATTLE THE BUGS AT CORTONDO GYM!

GO FUECOCO

TAKE ON A TITAN OR HEAD TO THE NEXT GYM?

I CHOOSE YOU, SPRIGATITO

TITAN

DEFEATED!

SORRY, BUG-TYPES ARE SUPER-EFFECTIVE AGAINST GRASS 'MON — OFF TO THE POKÉMON CENTER TO REST!

UH OH — THERE'S A WILD TERA POKÉMON! YOU...

RUN AWAY

CATCH IT

DEFEATED!

YOU RUN INTO AN EVEN STRONGER POKÉMON AND THERE'S NO ESCAPE!

TIME FOR ANOTHER GYM! HEAD TO...

CAN YOU COLLECT THE BADGES AND BECOME CHAMP?

FOLLOW THE PATH OF LEGENDS OR TAKE ON TEAM STAR?

TEAM STAR

YOUR PHONE GOES, IT'S...

NEMONA

LEGENDS

ARVEN

AZON YM

OPERATION STARFALL COMPLETED — WHAT'S NEXT?

DEFEATED!

YOU MEET A TITAN THAT WAS TOO STRONG FOR YOU AND ARVEN - TRY AGAIN!

BACK TO SCHOOL

POKÉMON LEAGUE

JAM

CHEESE

WHICH ELITE FOUR MEMBERS DO YOU WANT TO FACE MOST?

PICNIC TIME! PICK A SANDWICH.

LARRY AND HASSEL

RIKA AND POPPY

CARRAFA

EDALI

DEFEATED!

LARRY'S TEAM ARE JUST TOO STRONG FOR YOU TO OVERCOME — LEVEL UP AND TRY AGAIN SOON!

POKEMON CHAMPION!

YOU DEFEATED EVERY GYM, THE ELITE FOUR, AND TOP CHAMP GEETA!

Pokémon

PICROSS

CLEAR!
Pikachu
CAUGHT!

ART BY NUMBERS

In Pokémon Picross, you have to solve nonograms, which are a bit like crosswords but with pictures! As you work out the puzzle, you'll draw a Pokémon!

PUZZLE POWER

After collecting a Pokémon by drawing it, they can help you to solve puzzles with their special powers. What power they have depends on what their type would be in a regular battle!

DID YOU KNOW?

The first Picross game was Mario's Picross on the Game Boy back in 1995!

SUPER SOLVER

There are over 300 puzzles to solve, including lots of Legendary Pokémon and mega evolutions!

Pokémon PICROSS

PIKA!

RELEASE: 2015   PLATFORM: NINTENDO 3DS

PERFECT POFFINS!

RECREATE THESE TASTY POKÉMON TREATS!

YOU'LL NEED:

- 200g golden caster sugar
- 200g unsalted butter (softened)
- 400g plain flour
- 1 large egg
- ½ tsp vanilla extract
- Icing sugar
- Warm water
- Food colouring
- Sprinkles

ALLERGY AWARE!
Do not try recipes where allergies may be an issue.

Ask an adult to help!

1 Ask a grown up to preheat an oven to 180°C. Then, in a large mixing bowl, cream together the butter, sugar, egg and vanilla extract until fully combined.

2 Next, sift in the flour and mix until a dough starts to form. If you want to make your biscuits different colours, split your mixture into a separate ball for each colour.

3 Add a few drops of your chosen food colouring to your dough and knead until fully mixed.

4 Dust a clean surface with flour and roll out your dough to be roughly the same thickness as a pound coin, then cut out your biscuit shapes. We used an 8.5cm long piece of card to make an oval-shaped template for our poffins.

5 Line a baking tray with greaseproof paper, then place your biscuit shapes on top and bake for 8-10 minutes until the edges start to brown.

6 While your biscuits are baking, pour some icing sugar into a bowl and slowly mix in warm water until it becomes thick enough to coat the back of a spoon. Add a few drops of food colouring so the icing matches your biscuits.

7 Once your biscuits are cool, top with icing and sprinkles and leave for 30 minutes to let the icing set. Now it's time to tuck in, Pikachu style!

DID YOU KNOW?

You can feed your Pokémon poffins in Brilliant Diamond and Shining Pearl to raise their Cool, Beauty, Cute, Smart, and Tough conditions – perfect for bossing Super Contest Shows!

MIGHTY MOUSE!

DON'T LET THEIR SIZE FOOL YOU – THESE RODENTS ROCK!

RAICHU

MOUSE POKÉMON

PIKACHU

■ The most fa-mouse of them all, Pikachu stores electricity in its distinctive red cheeks, ready to zap opponents on the battlefield. Pay attention to its bolt-shaped tail – if it's straight across the top, it's a boy, but if it's curved into a heart-shape, it's a girl! But Pika isn't the only mouse in the fam, Pichu and Raichu are Electric mice, too.

PICHU

RATTATA

■ Despite their names, Rattata and its evolution Raticate aren't rats at all – they're both classed as mice! These cool critters are usually Normal-type, but in the Alola region, they're actually Dark/Normal-type and even have a totally different appearance.

PAWMI

■ Gen 9's newest mouse 'Mon, Pawmi, gives Pikachu a run for its money with shocking Electric power! Like Pikachu, Pawmi also generates electricity in its cheeks, but instead transfers the energy to special pads on its paws when it's ready to discharge.

SANDSHREW

■ Ground-type, Sandshrew, and its evolution, Sandslash, are another example of mousey 'Mon that had an Alolan makeover! It doesn't matter which Sandshrew you come across, both are able to blend into their surroundings and burrow for safety.

CYNDAQUIL
FIRE MOUSE POKÉMON

■ This Gen 2 Fire starter evolves out of its mouse classification when it turns into Quilava at Level 14. But before then, it has red circles on its back (kinda like Pikachu's cheeks!) that erupt into flame, making it look more like a hedgehog than a mouse!

BIDOOF
PLUMP MOUSE POKÉMON

■ Bidoof might start life as a fluffy-faced mouse, but when it evolves it turns into the Beaver Pokémon, Bibarel! It changes from a single Normal-type to Normal/Water-type and is able to swim with its webbed paws and paddle-like tail.

MARILL
AQUA MOUSE POKÉMON

■ This little blue ball uses its oil-filled tail to help it float in the water! Although Water/Fairy-type, Marill, might be an Aqua Mouse, when it evolves into Azumarill it transforms into a... wait for it... RABBIT?!

PIKA-WHO?

■ These Electric 'Mon might look like a certain someone... but there's not a mouse in sight!

MORPEKO
TWO-SIDED POKÉMON

TOGEDEMARU
ROLY-POLY POKÉMON

PLUSLE AND MINUN
CHEERING POKÉMON

DEDENNE
ANTENNA POKÉMON

TEDDY FINISHED RUNNER-UP IN THE JUNIOR DIVISION OF THE 2019 POKÉMON VIDEO GAME WORLD CHAMPIONSHIPS!

MEET A REAL MASTER TRAINER!

WHAT WAS YOUR FIRST POKÉMON GAME?

■ "Pokémon Sun and Moon on my 3DS."

WHAT DO YOU DO TO PREPARE FOR A TOURNAMENT?

■ "I find a good team, change it until I think I've got it at its best. Then practise lots with it."

WHAT'S YOUR FAVOURITE POKÉMON?

■ "Smeargle – I have used it very successfully in tournaments."

TEDDY'S TEAM!

HERE ARE THE POKÉMON THAT TOOK TEDDY TO THE TOP!

NECROZMA (DAWN WINGS) ·········· MAWILE

GOTTA WIN 'EM ALL!

DO YOU HAVE ANY OTHER PRO PLAYERS YOU LOOK UP TO OR WOULD LIKE TO FACE?

■ "Wolfe Glick (2016 Pokémon World Champion – Masters Division)."

WHAT'S THE TOP TIP YOU WOULD GIVE TO A YOUNG GAMER WHO'S JUST BEATEN THE POKÉMON LEAGUE AND WANTS TO START WORKING TOWARDS THE WORLD CHAMPIONSHIPS?

■ "Try to have fun and not get upset if you lose. Watch Pokémon content creators for tips. Every team has weaknesses – have plans to deal with them!"

DO YOU PLAN YOUR TEAMS ALONE OR DO YOU PLAY WITH A COMMUNITY OF OTHER PLAYERS?

■ "I usually build my teams on my own, using the data available from Pokémon competitions and my experience. Sometimes I team up with my brother."

WHAT MAKES POKÉMON FUN TO PLAY COMPETITIVELY?

■ "The community! You make friends seeing the same players at all of the events. Plus, you get to travel around the world for the different competitions and championships!"

GROUDON (PRIMAL) ...... **STAKATAKA** ...... **FERROTHORN** ...... **SMEARGLE**

INCINEROAR
THE HEEL POKÉMON

DOESN'T ALWAYS LISTEN!

+

✓ EPIC Z-MOVE, MALICIOUS MOONSAULT!

✓ BURNING BELT OF FLAMES!

✓ LOVES BATTLING IN FRONT OF A CROWD!

✓ INCINEROAR'S FIRE/DARK-TYPING IS TOO HOT TO HANDLE!

SPOT 'EM ALL!

There are five differences between these Pokémon moments, can you find them all?

POKÉMON GO TIPS & TRICKS!

BE A POKÉMON MASTER WITH THIS TOP TRAINER GUIDE!

Egg-cellent Incubators!

🔴 Blue Incubators break after three uses, so try to save them for 10km eggs. Use your orange Incubator for 2km, instead, to get the most out of your equipment!

Purify a Pokémon you've rescued from Team GO Rocket by feeding them Candy – they'll be easier to power up, too!

Get That Candy!

🔴 Transfer any Pokémon you don't need to Professor Willow in return for Candy. You can use Candy to power up or evolve the 'Mon you want to keep – EPIC WIN!

Be A PokéStop Pro!

🔴 When you visit a PokéStop and spin the sign, just hit the X at the bottom to close the Stop. You'll automatically claim all your rewards!

Excellent XLs!

🔴 Candy XL is unlocked after you reach level 40. The higher level a Pokémon is, the more likely it is to drop more Candy XL!

Use Lucky Eggs Smartly!

🔴 Save up easy evolutions for when you have a Lucky Egg – you can get tons of extra XP by evolving them in the 30 minutes while your Egg is active!

AWESOME INVENTORY!

BAG THE COOLEST ITEMS IN POKÉMON GO!

Pinap Berry

Double your Candy by feeding them to Pokémon before catching them!

Rare Candy

Rare Candy can be used on any species! Bonus!

Mystery Box

Transfer 'Mon from Pokémon HOME to Pokémon GO to get this exclusive lure!

Lure Module

Level up to bag Lure Modules to attract more 'Mon your way!

SURVIVAL CHECKLIST

TICK OFF EVERYTHING YOU NEED ON YOUR JOURNEY TO BE A POKÉMON GO PRO!

Phone ☐

To play the game – duh! It's also handy to keep in touch with friends and family while you're on the go.

Always remember to ask permission from an adult before you start your adventure and let them know where you are!

Portable Charger ☐

Keep one of these on you so your Pokémon journeys can last longer!

Snacks ☐

Nothing works up an appetite like catching Pokémon!

Comfy Trainers ☐

Your feet will be carrying you around on this quest so be nice to them!

Water ☐

It's important to stay hydrated!

Hat ☐

Not only will it help keep you cool, but it'll also make you look cool!

SEEING DOUBLE!

Are these famous gaming heroes trying to make their way into the Pokédex?!

TURTLEY FUNNY!

IT'S YOSH-ME!

SNIVY

YOSHI

JIGGLYPUFF

KIRBY

FENNEKIN

TAILS

QUAXLY

QUAKERS!

DONALD DUCK

'CHU WON'T BELIEVE YOUR EYES!

TOXTRICITY

SPYRO

JOKE ALERT ❗
What's better than one Pikachu?
Pik-TWO!

WHO'S THAT POKÉMON?

HOW MANY CAN YOU IDENTIFY?

WRITE YOUR GUESSES BELOW EACH POKÉMON AND CHECK TO SEE HOW MANY YOU GOT CORRECT!

1 This Pokémon's bite is worse than its bark!

____

2 Do you recognise this Water-type starter?

____

3 This Psychic-type Pokémon can deal some damage!

____

4 This super-powerful 'Mon was created as a result of experimentation.

____

5 This Grass-type starter is one of Ash's oldest BUDs!

____

6 These tapir-like creatures have a bit of a strange diet!

____

ANSWERS: 1. Fidough, 2. Piplup, 3. Farigiraf, 4. Mewtwo, 5. Bulbasaur, 6. Drowzee.

ALL ABOUT PALDEA!

THE POKÉMON LEAGUE

● The Paldea League is the only one so far where a person has been both a Gym Leader and a member of Elite Four at the same time! More than one person can also be Champion Rank at the same time in Paldea, so it feels a lot friendlier than other leagues.

CABO POCO

● After moving with your mum to Cabo Poco, you'll head out on your very own Pokémon school adventure! Will you pick Quaxly, Sprigatito or Fuecoco? There are no wrong answers on this test!

AREA ZERO

- A giant crater in the middle of the area! What are its secrets, and how is it linked to the Terastal phenomenon?

TERASTALLIZE!

- In Paldea, Pokémon can Terastallize! If they do, they'll start to look different and even change to their Tera-types! Be sure to pay attention to what's changed if you want your moves to be super effective!

MESAGOZA

- The biggest town in Paldea, with lots of different shops. You'll also find the academy here and can learn all sorts from its classes!

INLET GROTTO

- The Inlet Grotto is where you'll first encounter the Legendary Koraidon or Miraidon. Make sure you bring them a tasty sandwich!

WHO'S WHO?

BRASSIUS

★ Also known as the Verdant Virtuoso! He is an artist who is also the Grass-type Gym Leader of Artazon.

GEETA

★ The top trainer in Paldea! Also known as La Primera, she is the region's Top Champion and head of the academy's school board.

IONO

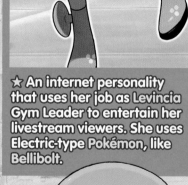

★ An internet personality that uses her job as Levincia Gym Leader to entertain her livestream viewers. She uses Electric-type Pokémon, like Bellibolt.

LET'S GET STARTED!

Get to know the Gen 9 Pokémon!

FUECOCO

A small crocodile creature that looks a bit like a ghost pepper! It often leaks fire from its small flame sac.

QUAXLY

A white and blue duckling monster! It has a large blue crest that looks quite a bit like a quiffy head of hair.

MELA

★ The leader of Team Star's fire crew, the Schedar Squad. She evolved loads of Charcadets in order to power-up the Starmobiles!

PROFESSORS SADA AND TURO

★ Sada and Turo are a pair of researchers that are regularly found in the Great Crater of Paldea, Area Zero. They're also your friend Arven's parents.

CLAVELL

★ The director of the academy and an unlikely ally! He's the one who gives you your very first Pokémon partner.

PALDEA

SPRIGATITO

A green cat-like Pokémon. It's a bit of an attention seeker, and can rub its paws together to make sweet smells.

MIRAIDON

One of the Legendary paradox Pokémon. He looks like an evolution of Cyclizar from the distant future. In Japanese Mirai means future.

KORAIDON

Another Legendary paradox Pokémon. It might be an ancestor to the Cyclizar we see today. Korai means earlier in Japanese.

Top Tera Tips!

WHAT IS IT?

● The Terastal Phenomenon transforms Pokémon, giving them a cool crystalised look and a shiny gem above their head called a Tera Jewel. All 'Mon in the Paldea region can Terastallize and their type determines their brightness and what their Jewel looks like.

TERA TYPES!

● When Pokémon Terastallize they don't just look pretty, but they get special powers, too! Each 'Mon has their own Tera Type that unlocks when they transform, as well as their regular type. This combo can totally change your team's strengths and weaknesses, letting you come up with awesome new battle strategies.

THE SAME KIND OF POKÉMON CAN HAVE DIFFERENT TERA TYPES!

AWESOME ORBS!

● Although every Pokémon in Paldea is able to Terastallize, trainers need a special Tera Orb, charged with Terastal energy, in order for them to transform. These Orbs need to be recharged after each use, either at a Pokémon Center or by touching glowing crystals that emerge from the ground.

RAID READY!

● You'll need to team up with three other trainers if you want to take down a wild Terastallized Pokémon! Tera Raid Battles have a time limit, so with three trainers battling at the same time, you need to work together to defeat these powerful beasts. If you win, you'll have the chance to catch the Pokémon in its normal form, as well as picking up some other goodies, too!

CRYSTAL CHALLENGE!

● Keep an eye out for colourful crystals as you explore – these are the key to starting Tera Raids. Each crystal shoots a beam of light into the sky, so you'll be able to spot a Raid opportunity from a distance. The colour of the crystal represents the Tera Type you'll encounter, so if you see a green crystal, you'll battle a Grass Tera Type 'Mon. This makes it so much easier if you're looking for specific types for your team!

CAN YOU FIND ALL FIVE DIFFERENCES BETWEEN THE TWO PICTURES BELOW?

POKÉMON SCARLET + VIOLET

SPOT 'EM ALL!

JOKE ALERT!
What do you call Sprigatito's reflection?

A copycat!

ANSWERS:

FEUCOCO'S COOKIES!

PREPARE A POKÉMON SNACK ATTACK!

PIKA-CHEW!

YOU'LL NEED:

- ⭐ Round biscuits
- ⭐ Mini marshmallows
- ⭐ Red food colouring
- ⭐ Chocolate chips
- ⭐ White icing

ALWAYS ASK AN ADULT TO HELP!

1. Split the icing into two bowls, with one bowl white and one bowl red.

2. Spoon the red icing on one half of each cookie, then fill the other half with white icing.

3. Pop a mini marshmallow in the centre of each biscuit, then use chocolate chips to make a line across the middle – just like a Poké Ball!

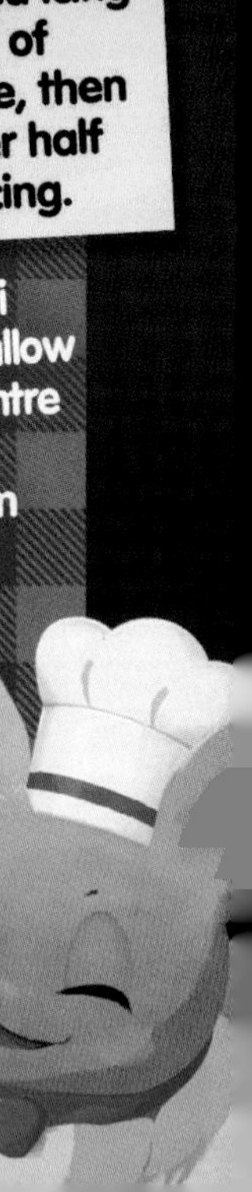

ALLERGY AWARE! DON'T TRY WHERE ALLERGIES MAY BE AN ISSUE!

FOLLOW THESE EEVEE PEASY STEPS FOR A TASTY TREAT!

Legend L

> SCARLET FOR THE W!

POKÉ POWER!

Depending on which of the games you pick, you'll meet either Koraidon in Scarlet or Miraidon in Violet. These super-mysterious Legendaries are said to be more powerful than other 'Mon!

WHICH OF THESE LEGENDARIES IS YOUR TOP PICK?

Fantastic Forms!

Koraidon and Miraidon can take on different forms so you can travel through Paldea in style!

SPRINTING BUILD OR DRIVE MODE

● While Koraidon uses its strong legs to sprint on all fours, Miraidon transforms energy from its neck and tail into spinning wheels to drive through Paldea.

owdown!

VIOLET FOREVER!

POKÉ TRAVEL!

Pairing up with one of these Legendary 'Mon will allow you to explore the open-world of the Paldea region in a whole new way, from flying through the sky to swimming in the sea! Who wouldn't want to go on an adventure with a Legendary Poké pal?

SWIMMING BUILD OR AQUATIC MODE

● Thanks to a special membrane between its toes, Koraidon can paddle through rivers, lakes and oceans, unlike Miraidon who relies on jet engines on its legs to propel through water.

GLIDING BUILD OR GLIDE MODE

● The tendrils on Koraidon's head can turn into wings that can glide through the air. Miraidon also uses its head to glide, extending its antennae and creating a thin membrane of energy - like a kite!

Pokémon PINBALL
RUBY & SAPPHIRE

LET'S PLAY BALL!

GOTTA CATCH 'EM BALL

You still catch and evolve Pokémon in Pokémon Pinball, but you do it by mastering pinball tables!

TOP TABLE

There are two main pinball tables to conquer based on Pokémon Ruby and Pokémon Sapphire. They're quite different, and you'll need to complete both to fill up your Pokédex, so don't just stick to one!

DID YOU KNOW?

The orginal Pokémon Pinball for the Game Boy had a vibration motor inside of its cartridge, so it rumbled as you played!

BRILL BONUS

There are even a bunch of bonus stages for you to try out, each themed around a different Pokémon, including Groudon, Kyogre and Rayquaza!

GAME BOY ADVANCE

Pokémon PINBALL
RUBY & SAPPHIRE

Nintendo 3+

RELEASE: 2003   PLATFORM: GAME BOY ADVANCE

POWER PROFILE!

POWER UP!

When Arceus uses Judgement, it's game over! They release countless shots of light with 100% accuracy and a Power stat of 100!

DAMAGE ALERT!

Like any Pokémon, Arceus has a type that they're weak against. If you're looking to defeat Arceus then a Fighting Pokémon like Machamp or Lucario will do the trick!

ARCEUS

DID YOU KNOW?

⭐ According to the Pokédex, Arceus shaped the universe with its 1000 arms!

⭐ Arceus is so strong that they can beat the trio that controls space and time.

⭐ Using the ability Multitype, Arceus can turn into any Pokémon type they want.

⭐ According to the anime, Arceus can bring back things they've destroyed – eek!

STATS:

STRENGTH	
SPEED	
AGILITY	
SKILL	
COOLNESS	

OVERALL ⟫⟫⟫ 9

POKÉMON LEGENDS ARCEUS™

BOARD GAME!

BECOME A EXPLORE HISUI AND SURVEY CORPS LEGEND!

START

ALL YOU NEED:
- A dice
- Coins or buttons to use as counters

1 JUBILIFE VILLAGE

2 OBSIDIAN FIELDLANDS

3 Commander has a quest for Kamado! Go back to the start!

4 HEIGHTS CAMP

5 THE HEARTWOOD

6 A frenzied Noble attacks. Miss a turn!

7 CRIMSON MIRELANDS

8 DIAMOND SETTLEMENT

9 You hitch a ride on a Wyrdeer. Roll again!

11 Alpha Onix is too strong! Go back two spaces.

13 GAPEJAW BOG

14 SLUDGE MOUND

15 You're moving up the ranks! Move forwards two spaces.

16 COBALT COASTLANDS

17 FIRESPIT ISLAND

18 You've gained Basculegion's trust; move forward one space.

19

33 You've completed the Pokédex, go to Mount Coronet!

32 PEARL SETTLEMENT

34 LAKE ACUITY

35 MOUNT CORONET

31 BONECHILL WASTES

36 You've found Arceus! Roll a six to win!

20 COBALT... HIGHLANDS

30 You spot a Zoroark run forward to the Pearl Settlement!

FINISH!

21 Miss a turn to help find the missing satchel.

29 ALABASTER ICELANDS

22 HEAVENWARD LOOKOUT

28 Ursaring attacks! Move back to Heavenward Lookout!

23 WAYWARD CAVE

27 Roll a five to get out of the space-time distortion!

10

24 Prof. Laventon is impressed with your work. Move your Mountain to Camp!

25 MOUNTAIN CAMP

26 Miss a turn to avoid the Alpha Crobat!

LEGENDARY TIPS!

Arceus

● You'll find the creator of the Pokémon universe in the Temple of Sinnoh once you've captured all the main 'Mon from the Hisui Pokédex. Use the Azure Flute to make Arceus appear and use balms to bring down its HP!

Giratina

● First, you'll battle this Ghost/Dragon type after facing Volo and his team but won't be able to catch it just yet. Luckily in Request 91: On the Trail of Giratina, you'll travel to Turnback Cave for your chance to capture this awesome Pokémon!

Darkrai

● You'll need to have saved data on your Switch from Brilliant Diamond or Shining Pearl to find this epic Legendary! Accept Request 93: The Darksome Nightmare on the Professor's board and head to Coronet Highlands where you'll be in for a tough battle!

Regigigas

● Visit Snowpoint Temple in the Alabaster Icelands. There's a door there that requires the Icicle Plate, Stone Plate, and Iron Plate to open. There you'll battle Regigigas!

Shaymin

● If you have saved data from Sword and Shield on your Switch, you'll be able to catch Shaymin! Just keep an eye out for Request 92: A Token of Gratitude appearing on the Professor's board after completing the main story.

Braviary
5/5
Braviary lets you take to the skies!

Wrydeer
4/5
Travelling across Hisui is much easier thanks to Wrydeer!

Basculegion
3/5
Basculegion allows you to surf across water to reach new places!

Growlithe
2/5
Growlithe will defend its pack!

THE DOS AND DON'TS OF...

POKÉMON LEGENDS ARCEUS™

How to ace your Galaxy Team missions!

DO

GET CRAFTING

Collect berries, plants, and other items to make useful things like Poké Balls and potions. You can buy items from Jubilife Village, but crafting will save you a lot of money!

BE CAREFUL WITH ALPHAS

Alphas are super cool and powerful! They make amazing allies if you capture them, and some drop rare items when defeated. If they see you, they're gonna attack so just make sure you're ready!

ACT SNEAKY

You have a much better chance of catching Pokémon when they don't see you coming. Distract them with food or stay hidden before throwing a Poké Ball!

DON'T

SWEAT THE POKÉDEX

Filling the Pokédex is important, but don't let it stop you from progressing with other parts of the story. You'll cross off entries quicker than you think as you battle and capture 'Mon on your travels. Enjoy the adventure!

IGNORE REQUESTS

Make sure to speak to villagers and complete their requests. Some offer small rewards, but others will upgrade Jubilife facilities like the local shop or farm which will definitely come in handy on your journey!

BE AFRAID TO RUN AWAY

Battles can be SO tough, even lower-level wild Pokémon shouldn't be underestimated! There's no shame in fleeing from a losing fight. That run button is there for a reason!

HOW TO BE A

 **CHAMP!**

2018 Pokémon World Champion Paul Ruiz tells all!

HOW LONG DID IT TAKE TO BECOME WORLD CHAMP?

"Six years. I started to play competitive Pokémon seriously back in 2012, mainly singles format. I started to play VGC format in 2013."

WHAT ADVICE DO YOU HAVE FOR POTENTIAL PRO GAMERS?

"Always put passion in what you do. If you want to get competitive, don't hesitate to search resources online and study a lot. Try to find friends you can practise with, and always try to find more information about the competitive game."

WHAT MAKES POKÉMON FUN TO PLAY COMPETITIVELY?

"The strategy – in this game you don't pick a character, you build a team. Even if you find someone using the same Pokémon, both can be completely different depending on how each one was trained, and that can completely change a strategy."

WHAT DO YOU LIKE ABOUT STREAMING YOUR MATCHES?

"For me, it is definitely interacting with viewers and sharing some of my experiences and knowledge. I really enjoy teaching others, that's why I became a VGC coach."

WHAT'S YOUR FAVOURITE POKÉMON EVER?

"Definitely Salamence. I enjoy everything about it: its design, its competitive aspect and its will to soar in the sky since it was a baby Bagon."

VICTORY – IT'S IN THE BAGON!

DID YOU KNOW?

PAUL IS FROM ECUADOR AND IS THE FIRST-EVER POKÉMON WORLD CHAMPION FROM SOUTH AMERICA!

TAKE A PIKA MY TROPHY!

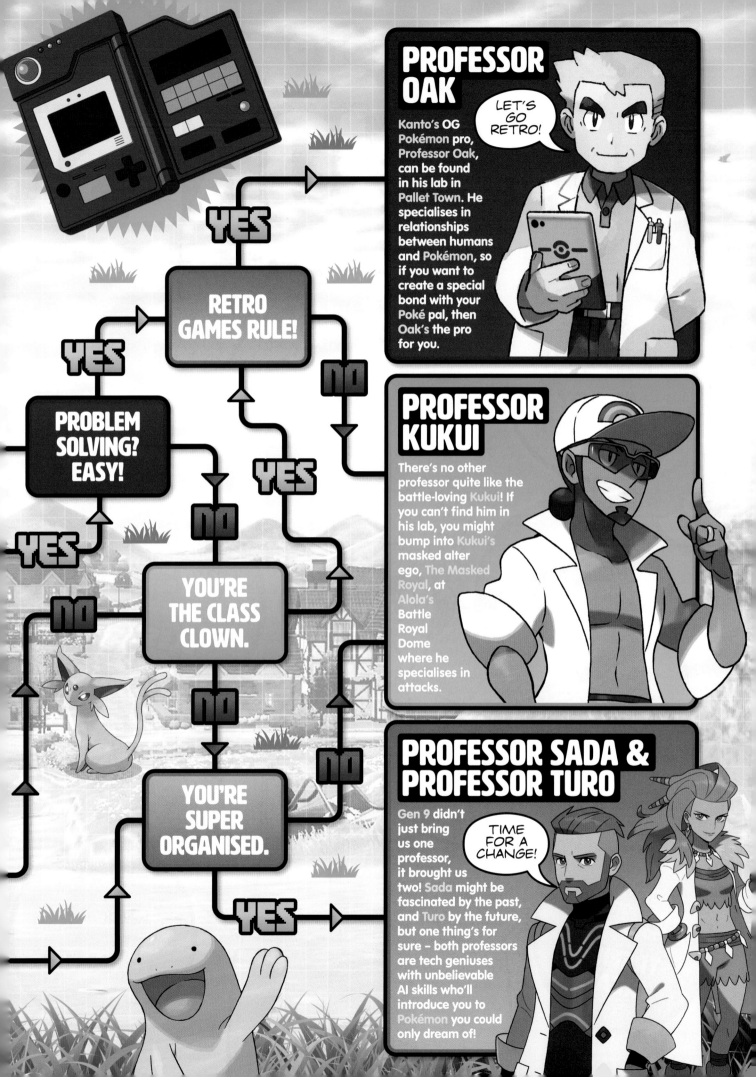

PROFESSOR OAK

LET'S GO RETRO!

Kanto's OG Pokémon pro, Professor Oak, can be found in his lab in Pallet Town. He specialises in relationships between humans and Pokémon, so if you want to create a special bond with your Poké pal, then Oak's the pro for you.

PROFESSOR KUKUI

There's no other professor quite like the battle-loving Kukui! If you can't find him in his lab, you might bump into Kukui's masked alter ego, The Masked Royal, at Alola's Battle Royal Dome where he specialises in attacks.

PROFESSOR SADA & PROFESSOR TURO

TIME FOR A CHANGE!

Gen 9 didn't just bring us one professor, it brought us two! Sada might be fascinated by the past, and Turo by the future, but one thing's for sure – both professors are tech geniuses with unbelievable AI skills who'll introduce you to Pokémon you could only dream of!

YES

RETRO GAMES RULE!

YES

NO

PROBLEM SOLVING? EASY!

YES

YES

YOU'RE THE CLASS CLOWN.

NO

NO

YES

YOU'RE SUPER ORGANISED.

NO

NO

YES

MAKE YOUR OWN
POKÉDEX!

Transform a chocolate box into the coolest Poké gadget around!

Ask an adult to help!

YOU'LL NEED

- A chocolate box with folding lid
- Coloured card
- Cardboard
- Scissors
- Sticky-back Velcro
- Colouring pens or pencils

1 Draw around each face of the box onto card and cut them out so you have a bit for every side. Draw around the front again to make a third rectangle.

2 Cut two of the big rectangles like in the picture. Stick the two big bits on either side of the box lid and stick one of the cut-out edges along the top of the box. Glue on the rest of your card strips so that the box is covered.

3 Cut pieces of scrap cardboard into rectangles that fit inside the box. Glue them all together and pop them inside. Now add a red rectangle on top so it's full.

4 Decorate another smaller rectangle of card with buttons and panels, then glue it to the bottom of your 'Dex. Use white and black card to make the screen and draw on the extra details before gluing inside.

5 Decorate the inside with more buttons and panels and add a blue circle of card to the top. We've used a strip of sticky Velcro to open and close our Pokédex!

EVERY TRAINER NEEDS A POKÉDEX!

TOP

MEGA RING

● Check out Mega Charizard! In Pokémon X and Y trainers have the opportunity to use a Mega Ring. These rings store Key Stones which, when a Pokémon is holding a Mega Stone, allows it to Mega Evolve!

POKÉDEX

● Created by Professor Oak, the Pokédex is a digital handheld database. It gives Pokémon trainers information about every Pokémon in the world. In Sun and Moon, a Rotom lives inside it!

TECH

POKÉ FLUTE

ZZZZZZ

● Wake up, sleepy head! By playing the Poké Flute you can wake up sleeping Pokémon! This is handy if a Pokémon is sent to sleep during battle, but it's also useful for waking up sleeping Pokémon like Snorlax, who block your path.

SNAG MACHINE

● This device is used in Pokémon XD: Gale of Darkness and Pokémon Colosseum. The aim of both games is to snag other trainers' Shadow Pokémon and turn them good again using Snag Balls. When a trainer is wearing the Snag Machine it can turn empty Poké Balls into Snag Balls.

NEED A HAND?

POKÉ BALLS

● You can't become a Pokémon master without Poké Balls! A trainer can carry six filled Poké Balls at a time – these are attached to a trainer's belt. Plus, there are different types of balls that can make it easier to catch certain Pokémon.

MEGA MEDICINE!

Keep your team in tip-top shape!

DOCTOR! DOCTOR!

POTION

Whether normal, Super, Hyper, or Max, the potion never stops being useful. Healing HP instantly can turn a battle around!

LEMONADE

Lemonade restores HP like a potion and can be bought from the many vending machines around the Pokémon world. Super-handy (and delicious)!

HAVE YOU GOT A BOO-BOO?

REVIVE

● Used to bring a fainted Pokémon back to fighting fitness, these can be given during or after a battle. Super-useful if you can't get to a Pokémon Center, especially in-between opponents at the Pokémon League!

ETHER

● These amazing items restore PP to moves allowing you to keep using them before a trip to the Pokémon Center. They're rare though, so save them for when you absolutely need them!

FULL RESTORE

● One of the best healing items to have! This fully heals your Pokémon and gets rid of any status ailments they have. Best used just before a faint to frustrate your opponent!

Some Berries also have healing properties! Turn the page to find out more.

PARALYZE HEAL

As you might have guessed, these cure Pokémon paralysis. With loads of moves causing this status, it is essential to have these on hand, especially at Electric gyms!

ANTIDOTE

● Although most Poison and Steel-types are immune to the effects of poison moves, the rest of your party might need some help. Use an antidote to avoid losing HP every round!

BRILLIANT BERRIES!

BOSS YOUR POKÉMON JOURNEY BY BAGGING THE BEST BERRIES!

Check out what these Berries do!

BERRY BOOST!

● There are two main ways to use Berries: let your Pokémon hold them so they use them when needed in battle, or give them to your Pokémon when you want to, like any other item.

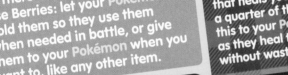

COOL COOK!

● Berries are one of the main ingredients in Pokémon snacks like Poffins and curries! In Sword and Shield, curries can boost your friendships, while Poffins can help you rule Super Contests in Diamond and Pearl!

SITRUS BERRY

● A very common Berry that heals your Pokémon by a quarter of their health. Give this to your Pokémon and watch as they heal themselves in battle without wasting a turn using an item!

CUSTAP BERRY

● Battles don't always go your way, but the Custap Berry is here! When you find yourself below 25% health, this Berry lets you go first on the next turn. Perfect for that last-moment victory!

LUM BERRY

● Having your Pokémon fall asleep, get burned, frozen, paralysed, or poisoned is never fun. Lum Berries cure all these status effects!

BERRY GOOD!

HIDE AND PIK!

CAN YOU FIND PIKACHU AMONGST THESE MIMIKYU?

WHAT 'CHU LOOKING AT?

ANSWER!

JOKE ALERT!

WHAT'S A GENGAR'S FAVOURITE FOOD?

I-SCREAM!

DID CHU KNOW?

PIKA PIKA! DISCOVER MORE ABOUT PIKACHU WITH THESE AWESOME FACTS!

FLYING WITHOUT WINGS!

Pikachu is the only non-Flying-type Pokémon that can learn to fly – they can learn it through special events!

FOOD FOR THOUGHT!

Ash Ketchum's Pikachu has a special liking for ketchup. In fact, Ash's Pikachu only seems to eat red food, like berries and red apples.

EVOLUTION!

Pikachu is the evolution of **Pichu**. Instead of evolving at a certain level, **Pichu** evolves through friendship and happiness. A Thunder Stone is needed if you want your **Pikachu** to evolve into **Raichu**.

PICHU
PIKACHU
RAICHU

HAPPINESS

THUNDER STONE

MASCOT MADNESS!

Clefairy was originally the mascot for **Pokémon**, but **Pikachu** ended up being much more popular. Poor **Clefairy**!

I CAME ALL THE WAY FROM THE MOON FOR THIS?

TELL TAIL SIGN!

Female Pikachu have heart-shaped tails!

BEAUTY SLEEP!

Pikachu recharges its electricity supply when asleep.

MAKE YOUR OWN PIKACHU EARS

● GET CRAFTING WITH THIS SUPER-COOL COSPLAY MAKE!

YOU'LL NEED

ASK AN ADULT TO HELP!

- Yellow card
- Brown and black pens
- Scissors
- Glue

1

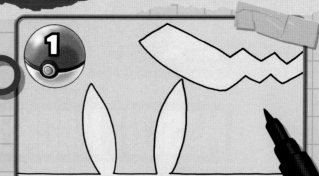

Draw a straight line across the longest side of the card, 2.5cm from the edge. Draw another line 2.5cm above the first one, then draw two ears on it. In a blank space of the card, draw a lightning bolt-shaped tail like in the picture.

2

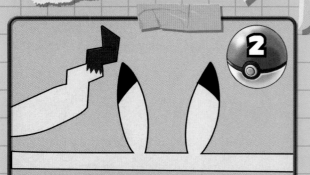

Carefully cut around all the lines so that you have one 2.5cm strip of card, one strip with ears and a separate tail. Colour in the tips of the ears with black and the base of the tail with brown.

WHO'S GOT POINTY YELLOW EARS AND A LIGHTNING BOLT TAIL?

PIKA-YOU!

3

Wrap the band around your head and glue it where the two ends meet. If it's not long enough, glue on the extra strip of card and trim it to fit. Add the tail to the back and you're good to go!

WEAR A YELLOW T-SHIRT AND ADD RED CIRCLES OF FACE PAINT TO YOUR CHEEKS TO COMPLETE THE LOOK!

PIKACHU'S CRAZY COSPLAY!

Get to know Cosplay Pikachu's five cool costumes!

Pikachu Libre can also be found in Super Smash Bros. Ultimate and Pokkén Tournament DX!

LIBRE
Watch out for Flying Press, this luchador wrestler-inspired Pikachu's Fighting-type attack!

ROCK STAR
Rock Star Pikachu doesn't just rock the mic, she also rocks the battlefield with her steely Meteor Mash move!

In the games, Cosplay Pikachu is a special female Pikachu variant with a black-tipped tail — the only known Pikachu with a tail like this!

POP STAR
Don't be fooled by her cute appearance, Pop Star Pikachu's Fairy-type Draining Kiss is a game changer!

Each costume has a different special move associated with it, but if Pikachu removes the costume, they forget the move!

BELLE
This Pikachu's icy blue gown is the perfect match for her special move, Icicle Crash!

PH.D
This smarty pants can super-charge the battlefield with her Electric Terrain, powering-up Electric-type moves!

Pokémon

TRADING CARDS!

Check out these powerful Pokémon TCG cards!

MEWTWO & MEW

This Psychic duo can use the attacks of any GX or EX Pokémon on your bench! Not only that, but with Miraculous Duo GX, you can deal a ridiculous 200 damage on an opponent – and heal yourself in the process!

SHINY MEGA GYARADOS EX

The shiny red variant of Mega Gyarados EX is a terrifying warrior you want in your deck! Blast Geyser takes a lot of energy to pull off, but it's worth it to blast your opponent right off the table!

PRIMAL KYOGRE EX, PRIMAL GROUDON EX, MEGA RAYQUAZA EX

This Legendary Hoenn trio come with matching cards!
Primal Groudon's Gaia Volcano can do 200 points of damage, while Primal Kyogre's Tidal Storm damages both your opponent's active and benched EX Pokémon.
Mega Rayquaza's Emerald Break does only 30 points of damage... But that gets multiplied for however many benched Pokémon you have!

MAGIKARP & WAILORD

The biggest Pokémon ever teamed with the most pathetic Pokémon have a Super Splash attack that deals 180 damage! Plus, their Towering Splash when combined with seven water Energy cards can do 100 damage to each of your rival's benched Pokémon!

TOGEPI & CLEFFA & IGGLYBUFF

The Rolling Panic attack already does a hefty 120 damage, but it has a lucky side to it – so long as you keep flipping a coin and getting heads, you can keep adding 30 points of damage!

TOP 10

REGIONAL REBOOTS!

⑩ ALOLAN MAROWAK

REGULAR TYPE: GROUND
ALOLAN TYPE: FIRE/GHOST

Thanks to the abundance of Grass-type Pokémon, the Alola region was a dangerous place for Marowak, forcing it to adapt and learn to control fire to defend itself! It's currently the only Pokémon known to be able to learn the move Shadow Bone.

⑨ GALARIAN WEEZING

REGULAR TYPE: POISON
GALARIAN TYPE: POISON/FAIRY

With top hat-like pipes and a green gas moustache, Galarian Weezing certainly looks different from its regular purple counterpart. This change in appearance was caused by pollution from Galar's factories, but Weezing has learned to filter the air, eating polluted particles and pooping fresh air!

8 ALOLAN MEOWTH

REGULAR TYPE: NORMAL
ALOLAN TYPE: DARK

Although Meowth also has a cool Steel-type Galarian version, we love Alola's sassy Dark kitty! Meowth was introduced into Alola as a gift for royalty, but this life of luxury was enough to transform Kanto's regular Meowth into the spoiled and cunning version that now roams Alola!

7 ALOLAN MUK

REGULAR TYPE: POISON
ALOLAN TYPE: POISON/DARK

Muk gets a colourful makeover in the Alola region! It even looks like it has sharp fangs and claws, but these are actually crystals of poison. These changes are due to the type of trash it eats, but beware – if Muk doesn't eat enough garbage, it'll go on a hungry rampage!

6 ALOLAN EXEGGUTOR

REGULAR TYPE: GRASS/PSYCHIC
ALOLAN TYPE: GRASS/DRAGON

There's a pretty BIG difference between Kanto's Exeggutor and the Alolan version! It's so sunny in Alola, Exeggutor kept growing and growing... and growing! Although its long neck can be used to inflict damage, according to the Pokédex, it can also make Exeggutor dizzy in the process.

5 HISUIAN GROWLITHE

REGULAR TYPE: FIRE
HISUIAN TYPE: FIRE/ROCK

Softer and fluffier than a regular Growlithe, the Hisuian version's coat helps it survive the tough climate. Its fur is also made up of pieces of rock, which is thought to have been caused by volcanic activity in the ancient region.

④ PALDEAN WOOPER

REGULAR TYPE: WATER/GROUND
PALDEAN TYPE: POISON/GROUND

Not only does Wooper have a brand-new look and type in the Paldea region, but it also has a brand-new evolution! Instead of evolving into Quagsire, Paldean Wooper evolves into the newly introduced Clodsire.

③ GALARIAN ZAPDOS

REGULAR TYPE:
ELECTRIC/FLYING
GALARIAN TYPE:
FIGHTING/FLYING

This Legendary bird has bulked up so much in Galar that it struggles to fly! Don't worry though, its super-strong legs allow it to run across mountains at over 180mph. Galarian Zapdos loves taking on tough opponents and is the only 'Mon who can learn Thunderous Kick!

② ALOLAN DUGTRIO

REGULAR TYPE: GROUND
ALOLAN TYPE: GROUND/STEEL

Alolan Dugtrio's distinctive bright blonde hair might look super-soft and shiny, but it's actually lots and lots of thin strands of steel – now that's a heavy haircut! Although these metallic whiskers slow Dugtrio down, they are great for defence and even help it dig through tough bedrock.

① ALOLAN RAICHU

REGULAR TYPE: ELECTRIC
ALOLAN TYPE: ELECTRIC/PSYCHIC

While Kanto's Raichu uses its bolt-shaped tail to harvest electricity, Alola's Raichu uses its more rounded tail to collect psychic energy instead. It can then use this energy to float, riding its tail like a surfboard! Many regional variations are caused by Pokémon having to adapt to the weather or the environment, but Raichu's transformation is thought to have been caused by eating too many pancakes!

DID YOU KNOW?

Alolan Raichu is the only 'Mon who can use the Z-Move, Stoked Sparksurfer!

FUN FACT!

Alolan Raichu's surfer design is likely inspired by Surfing Pikachu, a Pikachu variant introduced all the way back in Pokémon Yellow!

POKÉMON RANGER

THE FIORE FORMAT

Unlike other games in the series, Pokémon Ranger is mission-based, telling a story across ten main quests set in the land of Fiore.

GOTTA LEND 'EM ALL

Pokémon Rangers don't often catch wild Pokémon – they just borrow them for a bit with their Capture Styler!

マグマラシ

のこりじかん

00"16

GO-ROCK SQUAD

The Go-Rock Squad are bad guys that want to trick people into thinking that they're heroes! Can you stop them?

MIGHTY MANAPHY

You can unlock the ability to send the Mythical Manaphy to Pokémon Gen 4 games!

RELEASE: 2007   PLATFORM: NINTENDO DS

THE BIG POKÉMON QUIZ!

Are you a true Pokémon Master?

1 WHAT TYPE OF POKÉMON IS A TOGEPI?

A Fairy ○   B Psychic ○

C Water ○

2 TRUE OR FALSE?

Venonat evolves into Butterfree!

TRUE ○   FALSE ○

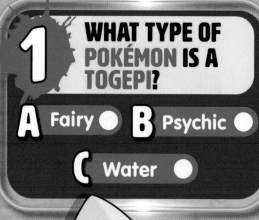

3 WHO'S THAT POKÉMON?

A Scorbunny ○

B Grookey ○

C Sobble ○

4 WHICH LEGENDARY POKÉMON WAS NOT CREATED BY REGIGIGAS?

A Regirock ●   **B** Registeel ●

C Reshiram ●

5 WHICH PROFESSOR GUIDES YOU IN POKÉMON SUN AND MOON?

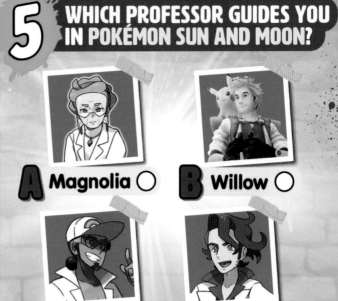

A Magnolia ○   **B** Willow ○

C Kukui ○   **D** Sycamore ○

6 WHAT IS THE EVOLUTION OF MR. MIME CALLED?

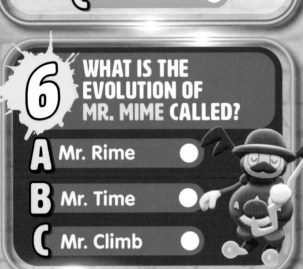

A Mr. Rime ●
B Mr. Time ●
C Mr. Climb ●

7 WHAT IS SPECIAL ABOUT THIS PIKACHU?

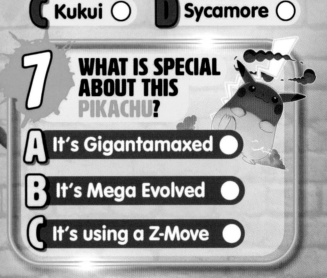

A It's Gigantamaxed ●
B It's Mega Evolved ●
C It's using a Z-Move ●

8 WHAT REGION IS LEON THE CHAMPION OF?

A Kanto ●
B Johto ●
C Galar ●

9 TRUE OR FALSE?

Every battle at the Pokémon World Championships is a double battle!

TRUE ●   FALSE ●

10 MATCH THESE GALARIAN POKÉMON UP WITH THEIR REGULAR FORMS!

Zigzagoon   Ponyta   Darumaka

A   **B**   **C**

GREATEST GROUND-TYPES

>> Who's your best battle companion?

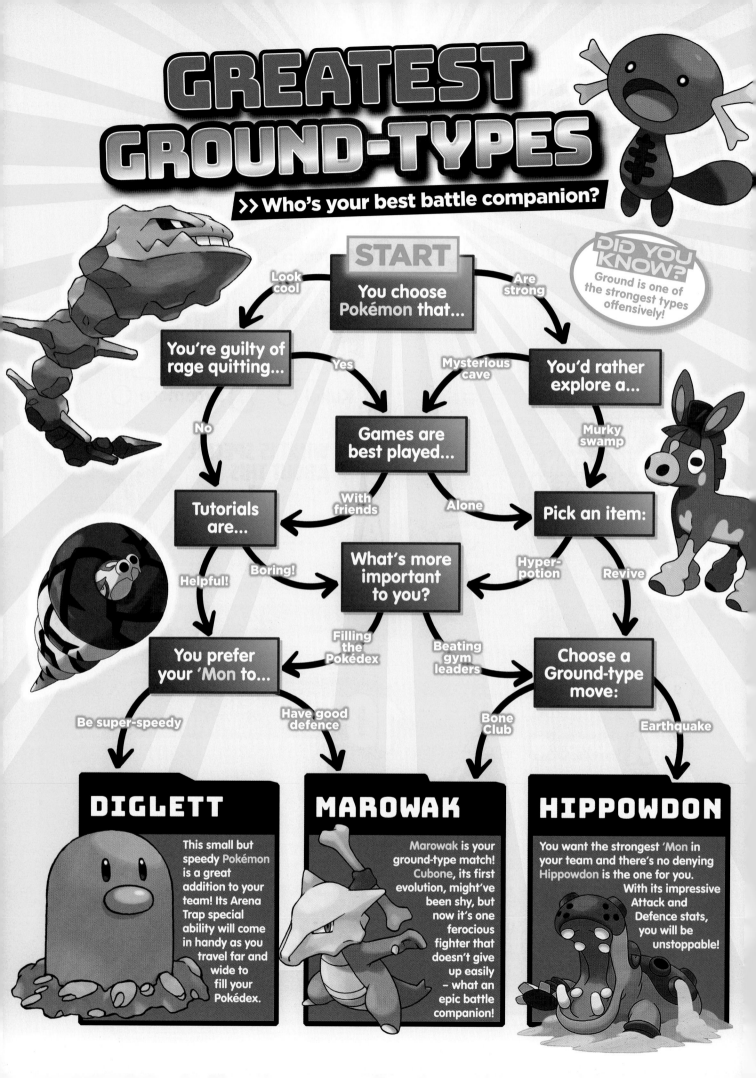

DID YOU KNOW?
Ground is one of the strongest types offensively!

START
You choose Pokémon that...

Look cool

Are strong

You're guilty of rage quitting...

Yes

Mysterious cave

You'd rather explore a...

No

Murky swamp

Games are best played...

Tutorials are...

With friends

Alone

Pick an item:

Helpful!

Boring!

What's more important to you?

Hyper-potion

Revive

Filling the Pokédex

Beating gym leaders

You prefer your 'Mon to...

Choose a Ground-type move:

Be super-speedy

Have good defence

Bone Club

Earthquake

DIGLETT

This small but speedy Pokémon is a great addition to your team! Its Arena Trap special ability will come in handy as you travel far and wide to fill your Pokédex.

MAROWAK

Marowak is your ground-type match! Cubone, its first evolution, might've been shy, but now it's one ferocious fighter that doesn't give up easily – what an epic battle companion!

HIPPOWDON

You want the strongest 'Mon in your team and there's no denying Hippowdon is the one for you. With its impressive Attack and Defence stats, you will be unstoppable!